The Real
Johnny Appleseed

Laurie Lawlor

Wood engravings by
Mary Thompson

Albert Whitman & Company·Morton Grove, Illinois

Also by Laurie Lawlor
• Addie Across the Prairie • Addie's Dakota Winter
• Addie's Long Summer • Daniel Boone • George on His Own
• How to Survive Third Grade • Second-Grade Dog

Special thanks to Professor Van Beck Hall of the Department of History, University of Pittsburgh, for reading the manuscript and making helpful suggestions.

Census data available in microfilm and early county histories of Massachusetts, Pennsylvania, Ohio, and Indiana—some of them published more than one hundred fifty years ago—were made available by the Newberry Library in Chicago and the library of Northwestern University in Evanston, Illinois. Some of these histories contain contemporary accounts and reminiscences that mention John Chapman.

PICTURE CREDITS

The cover and illustrations on pp. 1, 11, 20, 21, 23, 31, 36, 45, 48, and 51 are wood engravings by Mary Thompson. The map on page 6 is by Karen A. Yops. The illustrations on pp. 4, 10, 13, 15, 17, 18, 24, 30, 38, 44, 47, and 54 are courtesy of North Wind Picture Archives, and those on pp. 8, 32, 41, and 43 are courtesy of Cornell University Library; all are from nineteenth-century woodcuts and wood engravings. John Chapman's handwriting on p. 25 is courtesy of the Ohio Historical Society.

For Simba,
who has a special fondness for our apple tree

Here's to thee, old apple tree,
Whence thou mayst bud, and whence thou mayst blow
and whence thou mayst bear apples enow.

—old English song

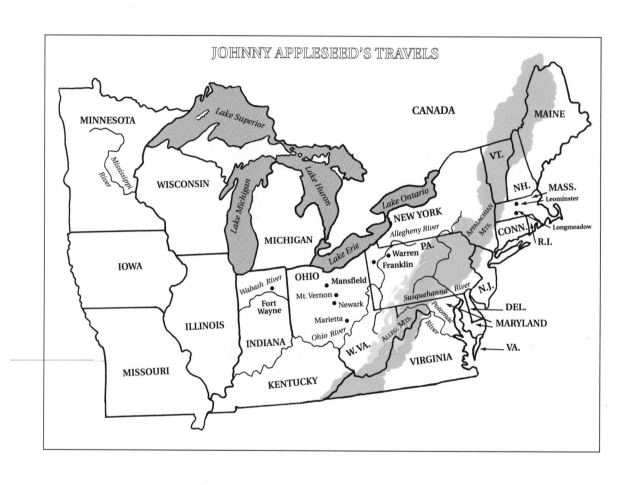

CONTENTS

*This earliest known depiction of Johnny Appleseed appeared in
H. S. Knapp's* History of the Pioneer and Modern Times of
Ashland County, Ohio *(1863). It is said to have been drawn in the
1850s by someone who had known John Chapman.*

The tale of American folk hero Johnny Appleseed has become a story that can't quite be believed yet can't quite be forgotten. He has inspired books, poems, songs, paintings, statues, plays, and festivals for nearly one hundred fifty years. In some accounts, Johnny Appleseed is an imaginary, raggedy, simple-minded wanderer in a tin mush-pot hat. In others, he is larger than life—a swaggering superhero who leapt icy rivers in his bare feet and crossed the American continent flinging seeds over his shoulders.

None of these images are true.

The real Johnny Appleseed was a flesh-and-blood man named John Chapman. He lived seventy-one years. Although his life was very different from his legend, he was truly a remarkable individual.

Uncovering the man behind the legend has never been easy. John Chapman did not talk or write about his childhood. He left behind no diaries, no personal letters. Not until 1939, almost one hundred years after his death, was information about his family background pieced together, thanks to the detective work of Florence E. Wheeler, a librarian in Leominster, Massachusetts. Because Chapman revealed few details about his apple-tree business to friends or relatives, it took years for researchers to add up all his land holdings. An incredible amount of this sleuthing and other Chapman research was done by Robert Price, who wrote *Johnny Appleseed: Man and Myth*. Other reliable accounts are found in land records, census data, early local histories, and letters and recollections of pioneers who knew Chapman. All of these resources were used to write this book.

Chapter 1

"The War Is Begun!"

JOHN CHAPMAN WAS NOT BORN IN THE SPRING WITH THE APPLE BLOSSOMS. He was born in the fall, when the orchards around Bee Hill and Chualoom Hill in Leominster, Massachusetts, were heavy with fruit and ready for picking. John's birthday was added to the record book kept in the Leominster meeting house, as was done for all Leominster babies as soon as they were born.

> John Chapman Sun of Nathanael and Elizabeth Chapman
> Born at Leominster September ye 26th 1774

As the clerk penned these words, he must have heard the clamor of voices and the thud of marching feet nearby. What was happening? In front of the meeting house in the muddy meadow called the "green," Leominster was excitedly preparing for war.

The militia drilled daily throughout September 1774. Drums rolled. Fifes played. Flags waved. Crowds from neighboring farms cheered as ninety-nine volunteers in every kind and color of homespun coat, vest, and breeches marched up and down with their muskets on their shoulders.

The Leominster Minutemen, as they called themselves, included more than half of the town's one hundred seventy-three boys and men between the ages of sixteen and sixty. They promised to fight the British "at a minute's warning."

Massachusetts was still a British colony. The people of Leominster and the rest of Massachusetts were ruled by King George the Third, who lived far away in London, and the royal governor, who had a grand house in Boston. Like all colonists, the people of Massachusetts were supposed to honor the king and obey the governor. For the most part, however, they had been allowed to govern themselves. In the 1760s, King George and his parliament had passed laws that taxed the colonists. The colonists had successfully resisted these efforts and remained suspicious of the plans of their king and parliament. They wanted to continue to make their own decisions.

In the spring of 1773, Parliament passed a law which changed the way tea would be taxed and shipped to the colonies. (Tea was a very important drink. Most people drank it rather than coffee.) On December 16, 1773, some Massachusetts men disguised as Native Americans crept aboard a ship carrying tea that had just arrived from England. These Sons of Liberty, as they called themselves, dumped ten thousand pounds of British tea into Boston Harbor to prevent anyone from paying the tax. This event, called the Boston Tea Party, was carried out with strict rules. The Sons of Liberty were not allowed to disturb any other cargo on board.

To teach the colonists a lesson, the British closed Boston Harbor and made an army general the new governor of Massachusetts. No ships would be allowed to come or go, the British said, until Boston agreed to pay for the destroyed tea. Boston refused, and produce

The Boston Tea Party

rotted on the docks. Then the British passed a law which prevented the people of Massachusetts from having town meetings or from electing many of their own local officials.

As months dragged by, the colonists remained determined to resist British power. On August 22, 1774, a group of Leominster citizens wrote a long letter to support their Boston neighbors. Before the letter was sent by express rider to towns across Massachusetts, the minister read it aloud. " . . . We must awaken and stir up every person to a thorough sense of the real certainty there now is of America being reduced to the most abject slavery and poverty. . . . "

"Huzza! Huzza!" the Leominster crowd cheered.

Colonists in Massachusetts and elsewhere now feared that the British might disband their legislatures and take away all their political rights. They called for a meeting of representatives from each colony to organize resistance to the British actions. These representatives, who met in Philadelphia in September 1774, were called the Continental Congress.

Of course, John Chapman was too young to understand this glorious, patriotic hubbub.

He was just a baby with blue eyes and straight black hair lying in a wooden cradle in his family's small rented house near the Nashua River. How could he know that among the marching Minutemen was his father, twenty-eight-year-old Nathaniel?

Nathaniel Chapman was a carpenter. Because he never made enough money to buy his own land, he rented a few acres. There he grew corn, potatoes, and turnips to feed himself; his wife, Elizabeth; their four-year-old daughter, also named Elizabeth; and their baby son, John.

After months of drilling, Nathaniel and the other Leominster Minutemen got their chance to fly into action. On April 18, 1775, Paul

Revere and other messengers galloped across the countryside to warn farmers and townspeople that the hated "lobster backs," as the red-coated British soldiers were called, were going to march through Lexington on their way to Concord. There, they planned to seize the colonists' hidden supply of gunpowder.

The Leominster Minutemen's alarm guns boomed on April 19, 1775. "To arms! To arms! The war is begun!" shouted a messenger on horseback. Men raced from their houses, barns, and shops. One Leominster Minuteman named Levi Woods became so flustered that he grabbed his gun and rode away, leaving in the field his small, astonished son as well as his team of oxen, still hitched to a plow.

That morning, seven hundred British troops reached Lexington and discovered seventy Minutemen already positioned on the town green. The battle that followed marked the beginning of America's

A Minuteman is called to arms.

fight for independence. Eight Lexington Minutemen were killed and ten were wounded before the British pushed on to Concord. Along the road more Minutemen and armed farmers and villagers hid behind trees and stone walls and shot at British troops. Before withdrawing to their ships in Boston Harbor, the British suffered nearly three hundred casualties.

Nathaniel Chapman and his fellow Minutemen marched as far as Cambridge, near Boston, but arrived too late to see the British retreat. Nathaniel didn't have long to wait to take part in the war. A few weeks later, the Second Continental Congress met in Philadelphia. It began to function as a government for the colonies. To fight the British, Congress set up a Continental Army with George Washington as commander-in-chief. Nathaniel enlisted as a soldier in the new army.

The Continental Army was undisciplined and rowdy. The men were likely to desert if they didn't like their orders. Congress had to constantly beg the colonies for money, men, and supplies. "Could I have foreseen what I have, and am likely to experience," General Washington confided in a letter to a friend on November 28, 1775, "no consideration upon earth should have induced me to accept this command."

In spite of these difficult conditions, General Washington did not give up. He managed to transform "the irregular mob" of men like Nathaniel Chapman into soldiers. Nathaniel fought in the Battle of Bunker Hill in June 1775, part of the struggle to end the British hold on Boston. In that battle, one thousand British were killed or wounded while one hundred forty American lives were lost. In August 1776, he witnessed the disastrous Battle of Long Island in New York in which more than twelve hundred Continental Army soldiers were killed or captured.

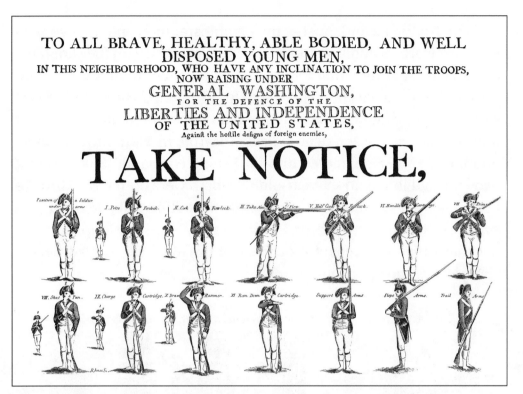

Part of a recruiting poster for the Continental Army (about 1781)

Because Nathaniel had a skill the army needed, he spent most of his time out of the line of fire. He worked as a carpenter, repairing wagons and building wooden fortifications. Soon he was named captain.

During the summer of 1776, rumors and false alarms flew. A smallpox epidemic was on its way to Leominster! British soldiers were coming to burn the homes and kill the families of every Massachusetts militiaman! So convinced were two terrified sisters from Leominster that they gathered their five children and huddled through a sleepless night with an ax, a sledgehammer, and two pitchforks under the bed for protection.

With Nathaniel and most of the Leominster men and boys gone to war, farmwork, in addition to endless housework, fell on the shoulders of Elizabeth and the other women. The crops had to be weeded and hoed by hand—a backbreaking chore for Elizabeth, who was pregnant with her third child. The Chapmans could not afford to buy a cow, "for they are very scarce and dear," Elizabeth wrote in a letter to Nathaniel on June 3, 1776. She greeted him as "Loving Husband." She said that two-year-old John and six-year-old Elizabeth were both well, "thro the Divine goodness." But her own health was failing fast. "My cough is something abated, but I think I grow weaker. I desire your prayers for me that I may be prepared for the will of God." She signed herself "Ever loving and affectionate wife."

The Declaration of Independence is read to a crowd in Philadelphia.

On July 15, 1776, crowds gathered on the Leominster green to celebrate the adoption of the Declaration of Independence in Philadelphia eleven days earlier. This document, which was written by Thomas Jefferson and approved by the delegates of the Second Continental Congress, announced the independence of the new United States of America. The people of Leominster were so thrilled by the idea that they entered their own declaration of independence from Great Britain in the town record book.

There was not much cause for celebration in the Chapman house, however. Nathaniel was still gone, for the war continued. Elizabeth lay in bed, overcome by tuberculosis, a disease that was destroying her lungs. She died July 18, after giving birth to a second son. John and his sister were now motherless. The baby, named Nathaniel after his father, survived less than a month.

With their father away at war, the children had to leave their little house by the Nashua River. For the next four years, it is believed, they lived with their mother's parents, who owned a modest frame house in Leominster. Grandfather and Grandmother Simonds, who were in their late fifties, had already raised nine children of their own when six-year-old Elizabeth and two-year-old John came to live with them.

Chapter 2

First Wanderings

In 1780, John's life changed dramatically. His father, now thirty-four, was officially released from the Continental Army. His last post had been in Springfield, Massachusetts, where he helped to distribute military supplies. That summer the war reached a critical point. General Washington's troops were hungry and ill-clothed. Some men were so starved that they roasted old shoes and ate them. It became more and more difficult for Congress to send men or money to the army because the new states could not agree on what each of their contributions should be. All remaining military supplies were considered precious.

Perhaps Nathaniel Chapman was dismissed because General Washington had to cut paid staff not directly involved in the fighting. One historian says Nathaniel lost his job because of "unsatisfactory management of military stores." This may have meant he stole army supplies and sold them in town for his own profit. Whatever the reason, Nathaniel Chapman found himself dropped from the army payroll on September 30, 1780, without a land bounty, a gift of land promised to soldiers who fulfilled their time of duty.

Two months before Captain Chapman (as he preferred to be called) was officially discharged, he married a woman from a respectable Connecticut Valley family. His new bride was eighteen-year-old Lucy Cooley, whose relations had been among the first settlers in the nearby village of Longmeadow. Sometime in the fall of 1780, Captain Chapman took his wife and children and moved out of Leominster. He rented a tiny, weather-beaten house at 135 Bliss Road in Longmeadow from one of Lucy's relatives. The house was one of the oldest structures in town. Like most buildings in Longmeadow, it was probably unpainted. Those few home owners who could afford the luxury of paint had but one color available: red.

Meanwhile, the conflict with Britain dragged on. It was not until September 3, 1783, and the signing of the Treaty of Paris that America finally won the independence it had declared on July 4, 1776. Eight long, hard years had passed since the first shots were fired at Lexington.

As the war drew to a close, the small house on Bliss Road had become very crowded. John's first half-brother (named Nathaniel, after the baby who died) was born in 1781; Abner arrived in 1783. That made four children and two adults. Two years later came Pierly, then Lucy, Patty, Persis, Mary, Jonathan, Davis, and Sally—a new baby every other year for the next twenty years. It was difficult for Captain Chapman, who worked as a carpenter and farmer, to keep enough food on the table.

To escape the cramped house, John probably wandered. Longmeadow was surrounded by wooded ridges and broad, open meadows. Outside his door to the east was a path known as "Way to the Woods." This crooked trail led to a forest of maple, birch, beech,

oak, and pine that had once been home to bears, moose, and wolves.

When John followed the road in the other direction, he came to the Connecticut River. Here he must have waded and learned to swim and to paddle crude log rafts. The river was the perfect place to watch the world go by. In spring, lumber was floated down from Vermont to shipyards on the mouth of the Connecticut. In summer, flatboats and barges carried goods to and from towns farther north and south. In winter, the frozen river became a broad highway from Boston for sleighs pulled by horses with singing bells on their harnesses.

Whether he liked it or not, there came a time when John had to go to school. By law, the town was required to hire a schoolmaster to teach the children reading, writing, ciphering (arithmetic), penmanship, and "decent behavior." Many students began as early as

A schoolmaster and his pupils in the early nineteenth century

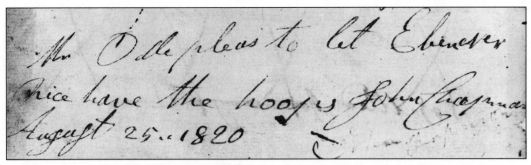

This note, written in 1820, is one of the few examples of John Chapman's handwriting.

age five. Children who had special needs, such as John's two deaf half-brothers, weren't allowed in school. These children remained at home and were taught by their mothers, if they knew how and had the time.

John learned his first lessons from a "hornbook." This was a piece of wood perhaps four inches long and two inches wide with a long handle that could be carried with a string. Printed sheets of text were mounted on the wood and protected with a clear covering made from animal horn, which is how the hornbook got its name. On one side of a hornbook might be the alphabet. On the other was the Lord's Prayer. The schools might also have had copies of texts like the *New England Primer*, which featured prayers and alphabet rhymes such as:

> In Adam's fall
> We sinned All.
>   and
> Zaccheus he
> Did climb a tree
> His Lord to see.

Because the entire school spelled and studied aloud, the roar of the students' voices was often so great that neighbors complained.

John learned to write using what was called "the Boston style." This rounded, uniform handwriting was easy to read. John's elegant, clear penmanship would serve him all his life. Like the other students, he used a goose quill pen with the tip carefully trimmed with a knife. The tip was then dipped into a bottle of ink. It took much practice to avoid making ink blotches and spots.

According to one half-sister, John became an avid reader and eagerly borrowed books whenever he could. But his schooling probably lasted only a few years. By the time he was fourteen, he could work for wages. He was required by law to give these wages to his father. John would have been "hired out" to local farmers to work in the fields and orchards. It may have been on some Longmeadow farm that John first learned how to plant and care for apple trees.

When he turned twenty-one, he could keep the wages he earned and go where he pleased. Favorable reports about rich, cheap land to the west had persuaded many people to leave Massachusetts and its rocky, overworked soil "for a new look out" in northern Pennsylvania. This area had been opened for white settlement in 1794, when a treaty was signed with the Seneca nation.

In the fall of 1797, John headed on foot for the Allegheny Mountains of central Pennsylvania. Now twenty-three, he stood five feet, nine inches tall and was described as "sinewy and large boned" with "remarkably keen, penetrating blue eyes." He wore no shoes. (The weather was very warm that fall.) He would travel three hundred miles alone with only his gun, small hatchet, and knapsack. In the knapsack he undoubtedly carried food for the journey, perhaps dried strips of venison and crackers. Soon the knapsack also contained something rather curious—apple seeds.

John collected the small brown seeds when he passed the cider mills in eastern Pennsylvania, where farmers brought bushels of ripe apples to be crushed into sweet cider. At the mills leftover apple seeds were free for the taking. Never a man to see anything go to waste, John probably gathered as many as he could carry.

Did he have a plan for those seeds? Maybe. Maybe not. Only one thing was for certain. As he crossed a high, broad Allegheny ridge in mid-November 1797, he was not thinking about apple seeds. He was thinking about the weather. Overhead, the sky suddenly darkened. Wind whipped through the trees. Snow began to fall.

To keep from freezing to death, John found shelter among some pine trees. He tore strips from his coat and bound them around his bare feet and ankles. Then he built a fire. After waiting out the storm, he waded through three-foot drifts to collect beech branches. He held them over the fire until they could be bent and woven into crude snowshoes. Using moosewood bark, he tied the snowshoes to his feet and was on his way, his knapsack over his shoulder.

After an exhausting hike, he arrived in what is now Warren, Pennsylvania, near the Big Brokenstraw River. It was fine country with plenty of chestnut, ash, and maple trees. In the summer, the river flats were covered with lush, tall prairie grass. When autumn came, the grass dried, broke, and fell over. The Native Americans had called the region Cushanadanga, "broken straw"—and the name stuck.

Although the American government had offered the land for sale to white settlers since 1794, there was only one cabin on the Big Brokenstraw when John arrived. John chose an open spot beside a stream, cleared away some trees, and planted his first batch of apple seeds.

No one knows exactly when John Chapman thought of planting apple trees for profit. But for an adventuresome young man without money, an apple-tree business made perfect sense. The seeds were free. The unclaimed land on which John planted his nursery did not cost him anything. (He was a "squatter," which meant he was farming land that did not belong to him.) From the time of planting, an apple tree might take seven years before it could bear fruit. The seedlings would be ready to sell earlier, however, when settlers came through this area of Pennsylvania on their way west.

Some settlers attempted to carry apple seeds or cumbersome seedling apple trees in their crowded wagons. Many of these trees did not survive the long, hard journey. A few pioneers found land with small, mature orchards planted by Native Americans with seeds brought from the East, but they could not count on this luck. John knew that farmers in a hurry to start their own orchards would welcome the chance to buy his young trees that required only a few years before they were ready to produce apples.

In some places farther west in Ohio, a company that sold land required settlers to plant fifty apple trees in order to acquire one hundred acres. It was a way to encourage "taming of the wilderness." But planting apple trees was also very practical. Apples were basic to the pioneer family's diet all year. (Other main foods were wild game and corn.) No other fruit could be put to so many uses.

In late summer, apples were eaten fresh. When fall came, they were buried in sawdust or stored in a cool, dark cellar until spring. Throughout the long winter months, apples were often the pioneers' main source of vitamin C. During the cold season, cut-and-dried apples hung from the rafters. They were "cooked down" (boiled with water) in big kettles and made into apple butter, a preserve that could be used all year. Leftover apples were crushed into sweet cider. If allowed to ferment, sweet cider became a popular alcoholic drink called hard cider. By boiling sweet cider, settlers created vinegar, which could be used for preserving cucumbers, cabbage, and other foods. On the frontier, vinegar and cider were often used like cash in trade for goods.

Wormy apples weren't wasted. They were fed to cows. (The problem was getting the cows to stop eating apples. A strong fence around an orchard sometimes helped. But a cow that ate too many apples became tipsy and didn't give as much milk as she did sober.) When an apple tree grew too old to bear fruit, the wood was good for whittling. Burned in the fireplace, apple wood gave off a wonderful fragrance on a cold winter night.

In lonely settlements, an apple harvest was a good excuse to visit distant neighbors. Around the time that John was growing his first apple trees, a Frenchman who had settled in nearby New York wrote, "In the fall of the year, we dry great quantities and this is one of those rural occupations which most amply reward us. Our method is this: we gather the best kind. The neighboring women are invited to spend the evening at our house. A basket of apples is given to each of them, which they peel, quarter and core. . . . When the intended quantity is thus done, tea, a good supper and the best things we have are served up. Convivial merriment, cheerfulness, and song never fail to enliven these evenings."

Settlers emigrating to what is now the Midwest (about 1800)

Chapter 3

"A Gatherer and Planter of Apple Seeds"

FOR THE REST OF HIS LIFE, JOHN WOULD DESCRIBE HIMSELF AS "BY occupation a gatherer and planter of apple seeds." What made his enterprise unique was that he never settled down. He moved his apple-seedling business west, skirting towns and cities—places that seemed to make him uncomfortable. Without a wife, family, or many possessions, he traveled light, always one step ahead of the next wave of pioneer settlement.

While John's first nursery grew, he scouted fifty miles up and down the nearby Allegheny River. Along the way, he met newcomers clearing land. In exchange for his help, John was given meals or a place to stay. One settler described him as "a mighty wood chopper [who could] chop as much wood or girdle as many trees in one day as most men could in two." Girdling a tree meant cutting and burning a ring around the base so that the tree would die and topple by itself.

Although John lived much of his life alone, he enjoyed the

company of others. He liked to sit at a settler's fire at night, sharing news and telling tales about his adventures. "He was a singular character," recalled R. I. Curtis, who was nine years old when John first stayed in his family's log cabin in Pennsylvania. "He was very fond of children and would talk to me a great deal, telling me of the hardships he had endured, of his adventures, and hair-breadth escapes by flood and field—some of them I remember."

During the next five years, John developed the work pattern he would keep all his life. Every fall he journeyed east to cider mills to collect bushels of apple seeds. He packed the seeds in leather sacks and transported them by horseback or canoe. After much scouting up and down streams and rivers, he located a promising spot remote from any settlers' cattle that might eat or trample the young trees. He cleared away trees and brush, built a rough fence to discourage hungry deer, and planted the seeds.

This depiction of Johnny Appleseed appeared in an article in Harper's New Monthly Magazine *in 1871. The article repeated many tales about John and made him famous.*

When winter came, he repaired his fences. Sometimes he chopped firewood or helped clear land of fallen trees for other settlers. Throughout the spring and summer, he traveled between his various nurseries in Pennsylvania and later in Ohio and Indiana, checking on his growing apple-tree seedlings. He cultivated those that needed care and sold the ones that were ready to be transplanted. His price for one seedling was a "fip-penny bit," about six and one-half cents. When he accumulated enough money from his sales, he began buying his own land.

While John was on the move, he visited cabins to advertise his business. If a buyer had no cash, well, that was all right. John was known to exchange seedlings for chunks of salt pork, a watermelon, loaves of bread, and even old clothes or shoes. If a family was too poor to afford his seedlings, he often gave them away. "He helped others more than himself," recalled J. H. Newton, who wrote the history of Venango County, Pennsylvania.

Venango County in western Pennsylvania was one of the first places where John set up his business. The spot proved to be a good choice. The state was encouraging settlement by offering one hundred acres to farmers who made a small down payment; cleared, fenced, and cultivated at least two acres; built a house; and lived on the land for two years.

As settlement spread, John's travels to sell seedlings became more extensive. He carried few personal belongings on his trips. He never seemed concerned about his appearance. To keep himself warm, he wore whatever was handy—a cast-off hunter's pullover shirt, two or three pairs of breeches, and a tunic made from a coffee sack. "Although often in rags and tatters, and at best in the most plain and simple wardrobe," remembered one settler, "he was always clean, and his most desolate rags comfortable, and never repulsive."

Just as John was not particular about clothes, he was not particular about hats. Anybody's old cloth or coonskin hat would do. For a couple of years he even wore an army officer's cap. But contrary to popular myth, no one ever saw John with a tin mush pot on his head. It is not difficult to see why. For warmth or as a sun shield for his eyes, a mush pot would have been an awful failure.

Constant foot travel meant that John only wore his precious shoes sparingly. To keep his current pair in good shape for cold weather, he spent as much time as possible barefoot. As a result, his feet became remarkably tough—"like an elephant's hide," wrote Abner Davis, who met John when Davis was a boy. "His feet were dark, hard and horny," another pioneer wrote. Talk spread (with help, no doubt, from John). His amazing feet became the focus of countless tales: how he walked barefoot for miles on snow or leapt across icy rivers. One account published in England in 1817 claimed, "He goes barefooted, can sleep anywhere, in house or out of house, and live upon the coarsest and most scanty fare. He has actually thawed the ice with his bare feet."

By 1800, John had several nurseries growing near the mouth of French Creek, not far from the trading center of Franklin, Pennsylvania. This region was perfect for his business. Every day settlers on their way to land farther west came through to restock supplies. The population in the surrounding county was growing. The census at the time shows one hundred sixty-one men living on claims. Of these, sixty-four were bachelors, just like John. Some of the men were trappers. Some were farmers. Some were drifters.

There were also many Native Americans living in the area. John moved freely among the Seneca and Munsee nations who came into Franklin to trade furs. He traveled with them on hunts, learned their languages, and adopted many of their methods of living in the woods. He learned which plants could be eaten when food was scarce and which could be used to cure ailments. He gathered wild catnip, hoarhound, golden seal, ginseng, and wood betony and exchanged them with settlers for a meal or lodging. Native Americans taught John how to hollow a log to make a dugout canoe, which he reportedly used on the Ohio River and later on one of his trips up the Maumee River in Indiana.

No matter how remote the backwoods he traveled, John was never harmed—even during especially dangerous times between Native Americans and white settlers. John respected the Native Americans, and they respected him. One of his favorite stories told how two young Native American men came into his camp one night to warn him of a nearby forest fire. They helped him fight back the flames and save his apple trees. In the process, they turned over a decaying log and uncovered a rattlesnake. The snake gave an angry shake. But the two visitors refused to kill it. "We walked around it with torches in our hands," John recalled, "talked to it and then left it to take care of itself."

Some settlers disapproved of John's spending so much time with Native Americans, who were often feared as "treacherous heathens." John did not think much of his neighbors' opinions. "He seemed to be as much at home with the red men of the forest as with his own race," one settler recalled.

When John turned twenty-five, he decided to set out for new country. Ohio was the place to go. As usual, he was one step ahead of other settlers in search of better land. In 1799, much of Ohio was still a wooded, hilly wilderness, criss-crossed by Native American trails and inhabited by wolves and bears. John explored the area as trails were blazed. Once four border scouts marking trails reported being startled by John's sudden appearance. John warned the men of hostile Delaware Indians in the area. Then he vanished between the trees. The story of his mysterious arrival and life-saving warning would be

repeated around settlers' campfires in years to come.

In 1801, John arrived in the Licking River Valley, a rugged area in the eastern part of central Ohio. His horse was loaded with leather bags filled with apple seeds gathered from cider mills in western Pennsylvania. He planted his first nursery in Ohio near the present-day town of Newark. This part of Ohio became the gateway to available land farther west. "Many earliest settlers recognized in him an old acquaintance who had wandered for years along the streams of western Pennsylvania, engaged in the same pursuit and preparing the way for those who might follow upon his trail to have their own orchards," wrote a pioneer from Knox County, Ohio.

Beginning in 1801 and for the next fifteen years, John expanded his Pennsylvania apple growing into Ohio. He planted trees along the Mohican River and Owl Creek in central Ohio, just east of present-day Columbus. In 1805, John's tales of rich Ohio land influenced his father and stepmother to bring their newest baby and half the rest of the family from Massachusetts. The Chapmans settled near Marietta, Ohio. (Captain Chapman would die near here in 1807; Lucy Chapman and some of the children remained, but historians know little about what happened to them.)

In 1806 John set up nurseries near the rough border settlement called Mount Vernon, thirty miles northeast of what is now Columbus. There were only a handful of primitive cabins built in Mount Vernon. The most prominent structure in town was a tavern. In 1807 the town was divided into lots to be sold to people who wanted to build houses or start businesses.

Sometimes a preacher visited Mount Vernon on horseback. But the effects of sermons on brotherly love were always short-lived. Corn whiskey flowed freely. Almost every day there was some kind of brawl. Crowds gathered to watch thieves being beaten with rawhide. Or they cheered as a wolf was skinned alive and turned back to the woods "to warn off the rest."

These crude forms of entertainment reflected the settlers' difficult lives. Every day was a struggle to survive. Clearing trees was constant, endless work. Winters were miserable and cold. Rain leaked through poorly constructed log roofs and made puddles on dirt floors. Wind and snow blew through unchinked walls. The settlers did not know much about sanitation and the importance of keeping their water supplies clean and unfouled by human and cattle wastes. There was not much nutritious to eat, and disease often wiped out entire families. The settlers' worst fear, however, was surprise attack from Native Americans, whose land they were now farming.

Border settlers in Ohio in the early 1800s

Unlike many men in Mount Vernon, John did not drunkenly shoot at Native Americans. He did not skin wolves for fun or profit. He was no swaggering braggart. And yet the settlers admired him for his stamina, bravery, and uncanny sense of direction in unmarked, often ferocious country. John mingled with the other settlers and was among the first voters recorded to cast a ballot in a local election. In 1809, he bought his first land—two town plots in Mount Vernon. He paid fifty dollars for the property. Although he kept the land all his life, he never built a house or lived there.

By the spring of 1812, rumors of scalpings, massacres, and revenge by both Native Americans and whites reached a fever pitch around Mount Vernon and nearby settlements. After years of bitterness and broken treaties, Native Americans in Ohio had been pushed onto one small northwestern section of land. This group, which included Wyandot, Shawnee, Ottawa, and Delaware, had joined under Tecumseh, a brilliant Shawnee chief. Armed with British guns and ammunition from Canada, these tribes appeared to be preparing for a major attack.

On June 18, 1812, war was declared between the United States and Great Britain, which still maintained its hold on Canada. Settlers in Mount Vernon and other Ohio settlements feared they would be massacred by British troops sailing from Canada over nearby Lake Erie. The more pressing danger, however, was the Native Americans, who had been armed by the British in order to eliminate the American settlers. "Blockhouses," often nothing more than reinforced cabins, were hastily constructed along streams, the easiest, quickest routes for settlers seeking protection.

Poor communication created many misunderstandings. Days could pass before news traveled across the state. The fastest way was to send a message by boat, but this was also the most dangerous. Tree-lined river banks provided perfect cover for ambush. To warn of attack, isolated settlers agreed to fire their guns in a special signal.

In the summer of 1812, John was temporarily living with a settler named Caleb Palmer. One day they were startled to hear three rapidly fired shots coming from the direction of a neighbor named Woodcock. This was the signal that there was an attack! While Palmer saddled up horses to escape to the blockhouse, John decided to find out what had happened. He disguised himself as a Native American, took his gun, and circled noiselessly around Woodcock's house.

Palmer waited. Three hours passed without any sign of John. Just as Palmer was about to give up and ride to the blockhouse, he saw something dodge between the bushes. A shape in red leggings! He raised his gun to shoot. At the last minute, he looked again. There was John, stepping through the trees with a side of venison. It turned out that Woodcock had not been signaling, but was instead shooting at a deer. John, who found him, helped skin the deer and was given a piece of venison in return. His red "leggings" were actually the bloody piece of meat.

Throughout the month of September, violent clashes between whites and Native Americans rocked the Ohio frontier. Atrocities were committed by both sides. In the settlement of Mansfield, not far from the place where John was taking care of one of his nurseries, an innocent old Wyandot was attacked by local soldiers. He was scalped and beheaded. His head was spiked on a pole on the street for all to see.

A few days later, the soldiers left town. Two warriors sought revenge by ambushing and scalping a white man on the west bank of Rocky Fork, just west of John's nursery. Ten families heard the alarm and scrambled into a Mansfield blockhouse.

Nobody knew when the rest of the Native Americans might attack

John warns Ohio settlers of attack by Native Americans.

again. Someone needed to warn other settlers still in their homes. John volunteered to make the dangerous thirty-mile trip from Mansfield to Mount Vernon alone. He saddled a horse and galloped through the night, telling settlers, "Flee for your lives!"

At dawn, he returned with reinforcements. The settlers in the blockhouse cheered. John was a hero!

Although there was no attack on Mansfield, killings of both whites and Native Americans continued. Indian villages and settlers' cabins were burned, and crops and livestock of both groups were destroyed. Settlers and Native Americans fled. When a peace treaty was signed between Britain and the United States in December 1814, most of the tribes had already left Ohio, never to return to the land they loved.

The violence John had witnessed during these years did not make him bitter or "war-crazy" the way it did some settlers. Instead, it may have prompted him in a new direction. He became an avid reader of the newly translated works of Emmanuel Swedenborg (1688–1772). This Swedish scientist and mystic wrote many hopeful books about God and how people might best live in the world. "Happiness is entirely within each man's grasp," Swedenborg wrote, "if he will only listen, reason, and apply himself to a good life." Swedenborg believed that every person must be of help to others in need. "The road to heaven is not away from but in the world."

At age fifty-six, Swedenborg wrote the first of what would become thirty thick volumes on his religious views. His followers based the "New Church" on these complex writings. In one book, Swedenborg described in detail how he found himself "to be constantly and uninterruptedly in company with spirits and angels, hearing them speak and in turn speaking with them. In this way it has been granted to me to hear and see wonderful things in the other life, which have never before come to knowledge of man, nor entered into his idea."

One wealthy Philadelphia merchant liked Swedenborg's books so much that he published seven thousand copies and sent them free of charge inside bales of cloth to customers all over the country. Perhaps it was while visiting a dry goods store in the Ohio backwoods that John discovered his first copy of one of Swedenborg's books.

John wrote regularly to Philadelphia for more books. Other

Swedenborg followers were impressed by John's ability to understand and discuss the new philosophy. In 1817, in Manchester, England, nearly thirty-five hundred miles away, a report was published by Swedenborg's followers describing John as "a very extraordinary missionary."

During the next thirty years, whenever John visited isolated cabins, he brought not only news, stories, and tree seedlings, but also books by Swedenborg. Sometimes he divided the books into sections to share. If the settlers couldn't read, John read aloud. In a time when few people could afford books, John provided one of the Midwest's first lending libraries.

John reads to settlers from one of Swedenborg's books.

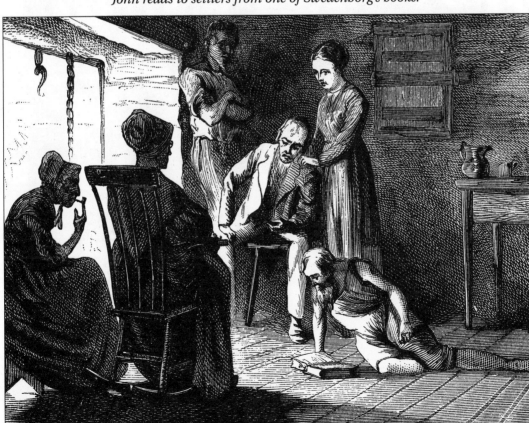

A cider mill (about 1850)

Chapter 4

John Appleseed

BY THE TIME **J**OHN WAS FORTY, HE HAD PURCHASED OR WAS RENTING MORE than six hundred forty acres of land in Ohio. As his travel circle became wider, he often needed help to care for his many nurseries. He hired William Broom, the husband of one of his half-sisters, Persis, to take care of some of his property.

In 1819, he hired two boys from the Vandorn family to help him clear trees and build a cabin in a swampy, wild piece of property near the village of Lexington, ten miles south of Mansfield, Ohio. The boys later wrote about this experience. Both were very nervous as they made their way through the dense forest. Where was John's camp? What if they couldn't find it?

Just as it turned dark, they spotted smoke. John stood beside a roaring campfire that was sheltered by a huge uprooted tree. "I never shall forget," one of the boys recalled, "how pleased he appeared to be when we came up to him in the wilderness four miles from a living soul but Indians, among bears, wolves, catamounts, serpents, owls and porcupines, yet apparently contented and happy."

After sitting down to talk, John poked potatoes from the ashes with a stick. The potatoes were to be dinner. "This is the way I live in the wilderness," he said, turning to his visitors.

"Well," one of the boys replied, "you appear to be as happy as a king."

"Yes," said John, "I could not enjoy myself better anywhere—I can lay on my back, look up at the stars and it seems almost as though I can see the angels praising God, for he has made all things for good."

In his fifties, John was described by S. C. Coffinbury as "a small man . . . thin in habit. His cheeks were hollow; his face and neck dark and skinny from exposure to the weather. His mouth was small; his nose small and turned up quite so much as apparently to raise his upper lip. His eye was dark and deeply set in his head, but searching and penetrating. His hair was black and straight which he parted in the middle, and permitted to fall about his neck. His hair . . . was rather thin, fine and glossy. . . . His beard was lightly set, sparse, and very black."

From 1820 to 1824, because of problems with claim jumpers (people who had taken over his land) and having too many loans he could not pay back, John eventually lost all his Pennsylvania and much of his Ohio property. But he refused to quit. By 1825 he was believed to have pushed west to Indiana. By 1834, he officially purchased his first Indiana land—one hundred and forty-two acres in Allen County for four dollars. Later he bought more Indiana land and set up additional apple-tree nurseries. Now his yearly travels took him in an even wider circle.

The farthest west he is known to have traveled was Iowa, although he never bought land or planted trees there. John Mitchell, a minister living in Whiteside County, Illinois, in 1843, recalled seeing John

Indianapolis, Indiana, in 1825

returning to Indiana from his trip west. John "passed through Whiteside County on foot and stopped at the home of a friend to stay all night. He said that he had been to Iowa, and that he was on his way to Philadelphia, to a New Church [Swedenborgian] convention." At the time, John would have been sixty-nine years old.

As he grew older, John did not settle down. His endurance remained remarkable. He continued to walk, paddle a canoe, or ride a horse great distances to tend his trees. "Straight as an arrow, slim and wiry as a cat," one person described him in his later years.

John spent the last twenty years of his life buying and leasing land and planting trees in Indiana. He was known as "John Appleseed" now. At a dry goods store in Fort Wayne, Indiana, on April 4, 1840, that was how his name appeared in the ledger for the purchase of a seventy-five-cent pocketknife. Nobody called him Johnny.

When he was sixty-eight, he made one of his last trips through Ohio and Pennsylvania. What had once been wilderness was now dotted with growing cities. While tending some of his remaining nurseries in Ohio, he spent as much time as he could visiting old friends and the families of his many nieces and nephews. Wherever he stayed, he brought the children of the household gifts of buttons, colored ribbons, and stories. Always there were stories.

"When I was quite young," Judge D. C. Carey remembered, "he stayed at my father's house clothed in rags and shoes bound on his feet with strings. He seemed happy and full of exhortation and good words. . . . He did not believe in fire and brimstone as a punishment for the wicked. He said he thought that the worse part of Hades would not be worse than smoky houses and scolding women."

When John journeyed to Fort Wayne, Indiana, in 1845, it was cold and rainy. After hearing a report that some cows had broken through a fence protecting one of his nurseries, he left the house where he was boarding. He walked nearly fifteen miles. When he returned, he went to bed, extremely tired. "A fever settled on his lungs, which baffled the physicians' skill," said William Worth, who owned the house where John stayed.

He died on March 18, 1845, when his trees were just coming to life again. On April 8, a local Indiana man wrote in his diary, "In the night thunder showers—then fair—first apple blossoms."

John was buried "respectably" in a six-dollar coffin. The man who made his coffin said that John was wearing "a coarse coffee sack slipped over his head; around his waist parts of four pantaloons; over these a white pair complete."

Most people would not have suspected that this kindly, shabbily dressed tree peddler was in fact a man who owned a substantial amount of property. John Chapman's estate included one gray mare worth seventeen dollars, fifteen thousand apple trees valued at four hundred fifty dollars, two thousand apple seedlings worth forty dollars, two town lots in Mount Vernon, and approximately eight hundred acres of prime land in Indiana and Ohio. In the course of his lifetime, he had owned or leased twenty-two properties totaling nearly twelve hundred acres.

In 1846, a year after John died, stories of his life began to appear in published local histories. Many of these accounts had been passed by word of mouth for more than forty years. John Chapman had become "Johnny Appleseed," memorialized as people remembered him in his old age: oddly dressed, homeless, religious—a wizened, ancient storyteller who remembered the days when the countryside was wilderness. In 1871, W. D. Haley brought Johnny Appleseed to national attention in *Harper's New Monthly Magazine.* It wasn't long before his legend captured the popular imagination.

Towns from Maine to Nebraska claimed Johnny Appleseed had visited and planted trees long ago. Poems, songs, novels, plays, and newspaper articles were written about him. Paintings, sculptures, and murals praised his deeds. He became the patron saint of American orchard growers and garden clubs. Schools, city parks, even streets were named in his honor.

Why has he become part of America's folklore? Perhaps because he was a real hero on the frontier. His work as a pioneer nurseryman symbolized the development of American horticulture. He unselfishly helped others at a time when many people were struggling to survive in a harsh wilderness. He was genuinely religious. He was a true character, an unusual man people did not forget when they met him. Perhaps the strong impression he made was due to "some rare force of gentle goodness dwelling in his looks and breathing in his words," as W. D. Haley wrote in *Harper's.* Haley claimed that even rough children

living in remote settlements would not follow and make fun of him.

In spite of all John Chapman's later fame, no one today knows for certain where his grave is located. His simple wooden grave marker has long since disappeared. But not far from the grassy hill two and one-half miles north of Fort Wayne, Indiana, where he was supposedly buried, is his best memorial of all. Apple trees. These trees, scattered throughout the area, are undoubtedly descendants of the thousands of seedlings John was growing at the time of his death.

FOR FURTHER READING

Bourgeois, Paulette. *The Amazing Apple Book.* Reading, Mass.: Addison-Wesley, 1987.

Chambers, Catherine. *Flatboats on the Ohio: Westward Bound.* Mahwah, N.J.: Troll, 1984.

_____. *Indiana Days: Life in a Frontier Town.* Mahwah, N.J.: Troll, 1984.

Franck, Irene, and Brownstone, David. *The American Way West.* New York: Facts on File, 1990.

Glubok, Shirley. *Home and Child Life in Colonial Days.* New York: Macmillan, 1969.

Helfman, Elizabeth. *Apples, Apples, Apples.* New York: Nelson, 1977.

Kellogg, Steven. *Johnny Appleseed: A Tall Tale Retold.* New York: Morrow, 1988.

Lindbergh, Reeve. *Johnny Appleseed.* Boston: Little, Brown, 1990.

McCall, Edith. *Wagons Over the Mountains.* Chicago: Children's Press, 1980.

McMillan, Bruce. *Apples, How They Grow.* New York: Houghton Mifflin, 1979.

Martin, Alice A. *All About Apples.* New York: Houghton Mifflin, 1976.

Patent, Dorothy Hinshaw. *An Apple a Day: From Orchard to You.* New York: Dutton, 1990.

Perl, Lila. *Slumps, Grunts, and Snickerdoodles: What Colonial America Ate and Why.* New York: Clarion, 1979.

Schnieper, Claudia. *An Apple Tree Through the Year.* Minneapolis: Carolrhoda, 1987.

Tunis, Edwin. *Colonial Living.* New York: World, 1957.

Tunis, Edwin. *Frontier Living.* Cleveland: World, 1961.

Watts, Barrie. *Apple Tree.* Morristown, N.J.: Silver Burdett, 1986.

BIBLIOGRAPHY

Adjutant General's Office, War Department, Washington, D.C. *Massachusetts Soldiers and Sailors of the Revolutionary War,* vol. 3, 333. Boston: Wright & Potter, 1896–1908.

Bailey, Frederic W., ed. *Early Massachusetts Marriages Prior to 1800 as Found in the Official Records of Worcester County,* First Book, 91. New Haven, Conn.: Bureau of American Ancestry, 1897.

Barber, John W. *Massachusetts Historical Collections.* Worcester, Mass.: Dorr Howland, 1839.

Baughman, Abraham J. *History of Ashland County, Ohio,* 110–15. Chicago: S. J. Clarke, 1909.

Block, Marguerite Beck. *The New Church in the New World: Swedenborgianism in America.* New York: Henry Holt, 1932.

Curtis, R. I. "John Chapman: Alias Johnny Appleseed." *Ohio Pomological Society Transactions* (Columbus, Ohio, 1859): 68–69.

Daughters of the American Revolution. *Lineage Book,* vol. 60, 159. Washington, D.C.: National Society of the Daughters of the American Revolution, 1910– .

Dirlam, H. Kenneth. *John Chapman: By Occupation a Gatherer and Planter of Appleseeds.* Mansfield, Ohio: Ohio Sesquicentennial Committee, 1953.

Federal Writer's Project, WPA. *Connecticut: A Guide to Its Roads, Lore and People,* 471. Boston: Houghton Mifflin, 1938.

Firelands Historical Society. *Firelands Pioneer* 5 (June 1864): 99 (Norwalk, Ohio: Firelands Historical Society, 1864).

Fischer, David Hackett. *Paul Revere's Ride.* New York: Oxford

University Press, 1994.

Fort Wayne, Ind. *Sentinel*, March 22, 1845 (obituary of John Chapman).

Graham, A. A. *A History of Richland County*, 266, 269–71. Mansfield, Ohio: A. A. Graham, 1880.

Haley, W. D. "Johnny Appleseed, A Pioneer Hero." *Harper's New Monthly Magazine* 43 (November 1871): 830–36.

Hedrick, U. P. *A History of Horticulture in America to 1860*. New York: Oxford University Press, 1950.

Howe, Henry. *Historical Collections of Ohio*, 431–32. Cincinnati: Derby, Bradly, 1847, and various later editions. See 1889–91, vol. 1, 260; vol. 3, 156–59; and 1896, vol. 1, 260; vol. 2, 484–87, 673.

Hubbard, Charles. *An Old New England Village*. Freeport, Maine: Bond Wheelright, 1947.

Journals of the Continental Congress, 1774–1789. Edited by Worthington C. Ford et al., vol. 17 (1780), 793. Washington, D.C.: U.S. Government Printing Office, 1910.

Kittredge, George. *The Old Farmer and His Almanack*. Cambridge, Mass.: Harvard University Press, 1967.

Knapp, H. S. *History of the Pioneer and Modern Times of Ashland County, Ohio*, 27–38. Philadelphia: Lippincott, 1863.

Meltzer, Milton. *The American Revolutionaries: A History in Their Own Words, 1750–1780*. New York: Crowell, 1987.

Newcomer, Lee. *The Embattled Farmers: Massachusetts Countryside in the American Revolution*. New York: King's Crown Press, 1953.

Newton, J. H. *History of Venango County, Pennsylvania*. Columbus, Ohio: J. A. Caldwell, 1879.

Nourse, Henry. *Military Annals of Lancaster, Massachusetts*. Lancaster, Mass.: W. J. Coulter, 1889.

O'Flynn, Thomas. *The Story of Worcester.* Boston: Little, Brown, 1910.

Peckham, Howard. *The Toll of Independence.* Chicago: University of Chicago Press, 1974.

Pencak, William. *War, Politics and Revolution in Provincial Massachusetts.* Boston: New England University Press, 1981.

Pierce, Charles. *A Meteorological Account of the Weather in Philadelphia from Jan. 1, 1790 to Jan. 1, 1847.* Philadelphia, 1847.

Price, Robert. "A Boyhood for Johnny Appleseed." *New England Quarterly* 17 (September 1944): 381–93.

_____. *Johnny Appleseed: Man and Myth.* Bloomington, Ind.: Indiana University Press, 1954.

_____. "The New England Origins of Johnny Appleseed." *New England Quarterly* 12 (September 1939): 454–69.

Report of the Society for Printing, Publishing and Circulating the Writings of Emmanuel Swedenborg. Manchester, England, Jan. 14, 1817.

Rice, Rosella. "Johnny Appleseed," in D. S. Riddle, *History of the Ashland County Pioneer Historical Society,* 165–73. Ashland, Ohio: Brethren Publishing House, 1888.

Schenck, J. S., and W. S. Rann. *History of Warren County, Pennsylvania,* 153–54. Syracuse, N.Y.: Mason, 1887.

Tanner, Helen Hornbeck. *Atlas of Great Lakes Indian History.* Norman, Okla.: University of Oklahoma Press, 1987.

Toksvig, Signe. *Emmanuel Swedenborg: Scientist and Mystic.* New Haven: Yale University Press, 1948.

U. S. Bureau of the Census. *Heads of Families: First Census of the United States, 1790– , State of Massachusetts,* 116. Washington, D.C.: U.S. Government Printing Office, 1908.

Vital Records of Leominster, Massachusetts, to the End of the Year 1849, 36–37, 127, 185, 256, 353. Worcester, Mass.: S. P. Rice, 1911.

Wheeler, Florence E. "John Chapman." Leominster 200th Anniversary, June 2–8,1940. Leominster, Mass., 1940.

_____. "John Chapman's Line of Descent from Edward Chapman of Ipswich." Introduction by Robert Price. *Ohio Architecture and History Quarterly* 48 (January 1939): 28-33.

Wilder, David. *History of Leominster.* Fitchburg, Mass.: Reveille Press, 1853.

Williams, W. W. *History of the Firelands Comprising Huron and Erie Counties, Ohio.* Cleveland: W. W. Williams, 1879.

Boldface page numbers indicate illustrations

ABOUT THE AUTHOR

Trained as a journalist, Laurie Lawlor worked for many years as a freelance writer and editor before devoting herself full time to the creation of children's books. She also enjoys numerous speaking engagements at schools and libraries.

She became interested in John Chapman because of her fascination with early American history. While working on *Daniel Boone* (a Booklist Editors' Choice for 1989), she first came upon folk stories about Johnny Appleseed. "Like Daniel Boone, Chapman was an individual whose life story was clouded with myth," Ms. Lawlor says. "What were these men, whom we know as heroes, really like? That's what I wanted to find out."

Ms. Lawlor's other books include *Addie Across the Prairie, Addie's Dakota Winter, Addie's Long Summer, George on His Own, How to Survive Third Grade,* and *Second-Grade Dog.* She lives in Evanston, Illinois, with her husband, son, daughter, and two large Labrador retrievers.

Library of Congress Cataloging-in-Publication Data

Lawlor, Laurie.

The real Johnny Appleseed / written by Laurie Lawlor ; illustrated by Mary Thompson.

p.   cm.

ISBN 0-8075-6909-7

1. Appleseed, Johnny, 1774-1845—Juvenile literature.   2. Apple growers—United States—Biography—Juvenile literature.   3. Frontier and pioneer life—Middle West—Juvenile literature.
[1. Appleseed, Johnny, 1774-1845.   2. Apple growers.   3. Frontier and pioneer life.]
I. Thompson, Mary, 1947- ill.   II. Title.

SB63.C46L37   1995
634'.11'092—dc20   94—22010
[B]   CIP
                                                                                                               AC

The text typeface is Utopia.
The design is by Karen A. Yops.